CW00958090

The Littlest Book of Bears

with 12 illustrations
by Ida Bohatta-Morpurgo
Written by Patricia Crampton

Ragged Bears

'Bears will be Bears'

When the sun is shining
Mother and Father Bear
go out for a walk in the warm hills, among
the summer flowers.
Little Growl is too young to be left
at home with brother Brown.

On Mother Brown's washing day,
Father Brown goes into the wood
to gather berries.
Father Brown would like every day to be
washing day.

Little Brown likes picking mushrooms,
but he has to take them home
to Mother Bear
to be sure he hasn't picked up
any poisonous toadstools by mistake.

While Mother Bear cooks the berries
Father Bear has picked,
Little Growl may get a nearly
empty honeypot
to finish off, if he is lucky.

"Can you teach me to growl
like Father Bear?"
Brown asks Mr Gruff, the choirmaster.
"Certainly," says Mr Gruff.
"Come and practise bass notes
after school tomorrow!"

"Isn't school fun, Little Growl?"
says Brown. "Oh yes, the breaks
are wonderful," says Little Growl,
"but I don't understand
what the lessons are for."

"I'm glad Mother asked us
to clean out the larder,"
says Little Growl.
"It sounded like hard work,
but it's the nicest game I've ever played –
even better than school!"

Poor Little Growl has a dreadful pain
in his tummy.
"What's wrong?" he wails,
"I've only eaten honey."
"Yes," says Brown, bringing
his little brother a hot water bottle
for his tummy.
But Mother Bear was not too pleased when
she saw that all her honey
had gone.

We know that Brown loves gathering
mushrooms,
but Little Growl is cross. "My basket
is empty, and yours is full.
You must have picked them all!"
"Try facing the other way," says Brown.

"If I climb a tree I shall see
all the mushrooms in the wood!"
says Little Growl.
But he is soon in trouble,
and brother Brown has to climb the tree
and help him down again.

Now that the nights are getting colder,
Little Growl decides he would be more comfortable
sharing Brown's bed.

Father Brown is already deep
in his winter sleep,
but Mother Bear is enjoying
a last read in bed
before she too falls asleep,
with Father Bear on one side of her,
and Brown and Little Growl
on the other.

The Littlest Books Collection

The Littlest Book of Kittens
The Littlest Book for a Friend
The Littlest Book Just for You
The Littlest Book for the Heart
The Littlest Book of Birds
The Littlest Christmas Book
The Littlest Book for Mother's Day
The Littlest Easter Bunny Book
The Littlest Book of Trees
The Littlest Book of Cats and Mice
The Littlest Book of Small Things
The Littlest Book for Every Day
The Littlest Book of the Way
The Littlest Book for a Joyful Event

Text © 1990 Ragged Bears Ltd
© 1990 ars edition, Zug in association with
Ragged Bears Ltd, Andover, Hampshire
Printed in Germany
ISBN 1 870817 45 1